WHAT TO DO ABOUT POLLUTION...

by ANNE SHELBY   pictures by IRENE TRIVAS

Orchard Books · New York

Orchard Books, 95 Madison Avenue, New York, NY 10016
Manufactured in the United States of America. Printed by Barton Press, Inc.
Bound by Horowitz / Rae. Book design by Mina Greenstein.
The text of this book is set in 28 point Leawood Medium. The illustrations are watercolor paintings reproduced in full color.   10   9   8   7   6   5   4   3   2   1

Library of Congress Cataloging-in-Publication Data
Shelby, Anne. What to do about pollution . . . / by Anne Shelby ; pictures by Irene Trivas.   p.   cm.
"A Richard Jackson book."
Summary: A very simple look at such problems as pollution, hunger, and loneliness and what can be done about them.
ISBN 0-531-05471-3.   ISBN 0-531-08621-6 (lib. bdg.)
1. Social problems—Juvenile literature.   2. Pollution—Juvenile literature.   [1. Social problems.]
I. Trivas, Irene, ill.   II. Title.   HN18.S527   1993   363.73—dc20   92-24173

For my parents

—A.S.

To Frost

—I.T.

What to do about pollution...

Stop it.
Clean it up.

What to do about
the hungry...

Feed them.

What to do about the sick...

Take care of them.

What to do about the friendless...

Be a friend.

What to do
about the sad
and brokenhearted...

Draw them pictures.

Tell them stories.

Sing them
songs.

What to do?

Love.